TERRIFIC
TENNESSEE

TERRIFIC TENNESSEE

Compiled by Ken Beck

PREMIUM PRESS AMERICA
NASHVILLE, TENNESSEE

TERRIFIC TENNESSEE by Ken Beck

Copyright © 1996 by Ken Beck

ISBN 1-887654-23-2

Library of Congress Catalog Card Number 96-71358

PREMIUM PRESS AMERICA books are available at special discounts for premiums, sales promotions, fund-raising, or educational use. For details contact the Publisher at P.O. Box 159015, Nashville, TN 37215, or phone (800) 891-7323.

Cover by L. Mayhew Gore Art
Layout by Brent Baldwin
Printed by Vaughan Printing

First Edition
1 2 3 4 5 6 7 8 9 10

Dedication

To my Mama, Hazel Rogers Beck, the best mom five kids could ever hope for.

And in memory of my Grandmother, Lois Knox Rogers (1910-1996), of Readyville, Cannon County, Tennessee.

Acknowledgements

Many thanks to those Tennesseans who helped with the compilation of these facts, especially Barbara Parker, Donna Pursley, Glenda Washam, and Wendy Beck.

Introduction

I was born in Murfreesboro, Rutherford County, Tennessee, in 1951, and I was reared the first two years of my life there and in Cannon County, where my mother's side of the family is Tennessee-born back to the early 1800s, making me a fifth-generation Tennessean.

Later, when I was growing up in Oklahoma and Arkansas, every summer our family would pack up the station wagon and make the long drive to Grandma and Grandpa's in Readyville, Cannon County. It was during these long summer vacations at my grandparents' rural home that I fell in love with Tennessee.

In the morning air there was a grand smell of a new day, and I recall barefoot walks in the dew-covered grass down to the barn to fetch eggs. At night you could see a million stars and catch a thousand lightning bugs, if you wanted. And those hours in between, from sunup to sundown, seemed to go on forever.

There were games of baseball, badminton and croquet; wading the creek; fishing for perch and brim; hauling hay; and corncob fights in the barn loft. But best of all, there was the river.

We lived every day to go swimming above the dam near the Readyville Mill on the East Fork of Stones River. After about two hours of pure lardy fun, we would hike up to Burnett's Grocery and spend our nickels and dimes on Cokes and candy bars. And 'round about 5 o'clock, Grandma would have a country supper, starring hot homemade biscuits like you wouldn't believe.

Those days were about as close to heaven as I figure a body can get. And those are memories I cherish. After I finished college in 1974, my love for Tennessee brought me back permanently; since then, my wife and I have chosen to raise our two children here.

As a writer for *The Tennessean* newspaper for nearly 20 years, I am fortunate to have been able to roam the Tennessee backroads from the Mississippi River to the Smoky Mountains to see the great beauty of this state and to meet some of its most unforgettable characters that make Tennessee what it is, a place I call home.

This book is a simple compilation of facts about some of the unique people, places and history of this state. It is intended primarily to be fun. What I truly hope is that those who peruse these pages will want to discover more about Tennessee as well as get off the interstate and head for the rural highways and gravel roads where the sights, sounds and smells are a delight to the senses and where the folks still sit in rocking chairs on the front porch and wave when you pass.

Go Tenne-seeing. You'll be glad you did.
And, oh, be sure and wave back.

Ken Beck

TERRIFIC TENNESSEE

1. Lucy Petway Holcombe Pickens, born in La Grange in 1832, is the only woman whose image has appeared on American currency (on $1 and $100 Confederate notes).

2. There are 31 bicentennial farms in Tennessee, meaning farms that have been in the same family for at least 200 years. The oldest farm in the state, Greene County's Elmwood Farm, is owned by Claudius and Katherine Earnest Clemmer and has been in Katherine's family since 1777.

3. The *Memphis Belle* was the first B-17 bomber to fly 25 combat missions over Nazi-occupied Europe during World War II. The plane is now displayed on Mud Island in the Mississippi River at Memphis.

4. On Highway 51 in West Tennessee, a series of communities along the beaten path helped create the saying "Down the Halls, through the Gates, around the Curve, and Flippin' into Ripley."

TERRIFIC TENNESSEE

5. Clarksville's Wilma Rudolph was the first American woman to win three gold medals at one Olympics (1960). As a child she suffered from polio and wore leg braces.

6. The first auto manufactured in the South was the Marathon, made in Jackson in 1907 and then in Nashville from 1910 to 1914. About 10,000 of the autos were made but only eight exist today. Its Nashville assembly plant, Marathon Village, has been the site for 150 country music videos.

7. The world's largest red cedar bucket was made in 1887 in Murfreesboro. The 2,000-gallon bucket may be seen in Cannonsburgh. Please don't kick the bucket.

8. Some pennies come from heaven, but most of them come from the Zinc Products Co. in Greeneville. The company produces copper-coated blank zinc coins that account for nearly 85% of the 13.5 billion pennies made annually. That makes cents.

TERRIFIC TENNESSEE

9. The largest pig of all time was a Weakley County porker, the 2,552-pound Poland-China hog, Big Bill. Big Bill was nearly nine feet long and about four and a half feet tall when he died in 1933. His owner, Walter Jackson Chappell of Martin, had him stuffed and displayed until 1946 when Big Bill was sold to a carnival. Bill's diet was corn meal and sorghum molasses. That hog was some hoss.

10. NASCAR driver Sterling Marlin of Carter's Creek won the 1994 and 1995 Daytona 500 titles.

11. W.C. (William Christopher) Handy, father of the blues, wrote *The Beale Street Blues* in 1909 as a campaign song for Memphis political leader E.H. "Boss" Crump. It became such a hit that Handy turned it into *The Memphis Blues*, the first blues ever published. Handy's statue stands today on Beale Street and his home is now the W.C. Handy Museum. He was honored on a postage stamp in 1969.

TERRIFIC TENNESSEE

12. Krystal's famous burgers first felt the mustard in Chattanooga in 1932. The price for this Chattanooga chew-chew: a nickel.

13. Sgt. Alvin C. York, a pacifist from Pall Mall, earned more than 40 military decorations for his feat on Oct. 8, 1918, when he shot 25 German soldiers and captured 132 prisoners in the Argonne Forest of France. He was portrayed by Gary Cooper in the film *Sergeant York*. You can chat with York's son, Andrew, a park ranger, almost any day at the historic Alvin C. York Grist Mill and Park in Pall Mall, several miles north of Jamestown.

14. The Tennessee Aquarium in Chattanooga has a 61-pound, 43-inch-long blue catfish that is believed to be the largest live catfish in a U.S. zoo or aquarium. It was caught in a TVA pumped-storage reservoir atop Raccoon Mountain. The largest known blue catfish caught in the state was a 130-pounder fished from the Fort Loudon Reservoir in 1976.

TERRIFIC TENNESSEE

15. Tennessee is the only state that has issued auto license plates shaped like the state (1936-1956). Today you can have an iris, a bluebird, a fish or a swinging cat on your plate.

16. Miniature golf was invented in the late 1920s atop Lookout Mountain by Garnet Carter, who built the Tom Thumb course at the Fairyland Inn for his wife. Among those who came to putter around were Babe Ruth and Bobby Jones.

17. David Crockett was born Aug. 17, 1786, in Limestone. The hunter, humorist, politician and war hero died at the Alamo. His motto: "Be always sure you're right—then go ahead!"

18. The first black artist to have a one-man show at the Museum of Modern Art in New York City (1937) was Nashville sculptor William Edmondson. His primitive limestone carvings included angels, biblical characters and Eleanor Roosevelt.

TERRIFIC TENNESSEE

19. Rambling man and guitar picker Gregg Allman, one of the Allman Brothers of Southern rock fame, was born Dec. 8, 1947, in Nashville.

20. Hattie Harrison Gaddis, who was born in Greene County in 1894 and became known as "Mammy" Gaddis, was a midwife who delivered around 700 babies over a span of 45 years, losing only two. She charged no fee but husbands of her patients spent a day working for "Pap" Gaddis on the family farm.

21. Country music superstar Dolly Parton was born Jan. 19, 1946, in Locust Ridge, near Sevierville, the fourth of 12 children. The singer-songwriter-actress built Dollywood near Pigeon Forge in 1986. She is famous for two other reasons, but I forget.

22. The Natchez Trace Parkway Bridge, which crosses over Highway 96 in Williamson County, is the largest segmented, arched bridge in the United States.

TERRIFIC TENNESSEE

23. The mascot of Cumberland University in Lebanon was a bulldog named Rascal, who from 1931 to 1940 attended every law class at the school's Caruthers Hall. When the dog died he was buried with ceremony beside the building and a stone marking his grave read: "Here lies Rascal L.L.B. Attended C.U. Law School 9 yrs, crossed the bar 1940."

24. South Fulton, which for 60 years was the redistribution center for 70% of all bananas brought into the U.S., hosts an annual International Banana Festival each September that features a one-ton banana pudding. Don't slip.

25. The first air mail with letters bearing an adhesive postage stamp was delivered from Nashville to Gallatin on June 17, 1877, by Samuel Archer King in his hot air balloon, the *Buffalo*. Each letter bore a 5-cent stamp. Nashville's Cumberland Park was the site of takeoff for the world's first night airplane flight on June 22, 1910, when Charles K. Hamilton took off at 10:57 p.m. and soared for 18 minutes.

TERRIFIC TENNESSEE

26. The world's largest watermelon, a 262-pound whopper, was grown in Arrington in 1990 by Bill Carson. Whattamelon.

27. Andrew Jackson was a notoriously bad speller. As prosecuting attorney of Davidson County he would approve court records by writing Oll Korrect on the papers. When that became tiresome, he started signing the papers with "O.K.", and thus the word okay was coined.

28. "Roasted 'possum with sweet potatoes is a prime Tennessee dish. ... In some sections of the State 'possum and 'taters are canned."—*The WPA Guide to Tennessee,* 1939

"Not anymore."—*Terrific Tennessee,* 1996

29. More than nine million Christmas trees are grown in Tennessee, including white pine, Virginia pine, Fraser fir, Norway spruce and blue spruce. Come and get it, Charlie Brown.

30. The world-record smallmouth bass, a 10-pound, 8-ounce lunker, was caught by Paul E. Beal in Hendrick Creek of Dale Hollow Lake in 1986. That smallmouth had too big a mouth.

31. The Goo Goo candy bar, the world's first combination candy bar, was invented in Nashville in 1912 by Howell Campbell and Porter Moore. It's gooooood. The same company, Standard, has been making King Leo pure cane sugar sticks, "the candy that roars with flavor," since 1901. How sweet it is!

32. The first time Coca-Cola became a bottle of pop was in 1899 in Chattanooga. Wonder what people put their Tom's Peanuts in before then?

33. The socks that astronauts Aldrin and Armstrong wore when they walked on the moon were made by Nashville's May Hosiery Mills. They had no problem with athlete's foot but had to remain wary of "missile toe."

TERRIFIC TENNESSEE

34. Buford Pusser was the 6-foot-6-tall sheriff of McNairy County who carried a big stick and became even more famous after three *Walking Tall* films. The lawman was shot eight times and knifed seven times, and his house in Adamsville is now a museum honoring him.

35. The only arrest for witchcraft made in the state was in Fentress County in 1835 when a posse armed with guns loaded with silver bullets arrested a reclusive old man named Joseph Stout. He was found innocent.

36. Songwriter-poet James Weldon Johnson was a professor at Fisk University during the 1930s. He wrote *Lift Every Voice and Sing*, which was considered the black national anthem in the early part of this century.

37. Tennessee State University's legendary track coach Ed Temple trained 40 Olympic athletes during his lengthy career and saw his athletes win 23 medals and 13 gold medals at the Olympics.

TERRIFIC TENNESSEE

38. Among national TV series filmed in Tennessee were *Christy, Nashville 99, Hee Haw, I-40 Paradise* and portions of Disney's *Davy Crockett* miniseries. TV series that were set in Tennessee include *Casey Jones, Boone* and *Palmerstown.*

39. Joe Walker, born Joseph Reddeford Walker on Dec. 13, 1798, in Roane County, was known as "the king of the trailblazers." The ideal mountain man, Walker led the group who became the first white men to see Yosemite Valley and the giant redwood trees of California.

40. Bakersville native Comdr. William R. Anderson was the first man to skipper the atomic-powered submarine *Nautilus* from the Pacific Ocean to the Atlantic Ocean via the Arctic Ocean and underneath the polar ice pack. The most acclaimed naval hero since World War II took his sub beneath the North Pole on Aug. 3, 1958. In honor of the event, the town of Waverly named its hospital after the submarine.

41. Mills Darden (1799-1857) of Henderson County was the biggest Tennessean of them all. He weighed 1,020 pounds and stood seven feet, six inches tall. It took 17 men to place him in his "coffin," which was made from 500 board feet of lumber. The second tallest man in the world was Gallatin's John William Rogan (1871-1905), who was eight feet, eight inches tall and weighed 175 pounds. Rogan was measured sitting down because he could not stand.

42. The state songs include *My Homeland, Tennessee* (1925); *When It's Iris Time in Tennessee* (1935); *My Tennessee* (1955); *Tennessee Waltz* (1965); and *Rocky Top* (1982). Just call us singing fools.

43. Since Nov. 28, 1925, the Grand Ole Opry has been broadcast over WSM every Saturday night, making it the longest continuing live radio program in the U.S. Its first performer was fiddler Uncle Jimmy Thompson. Like the solemn ole judge said, "Let her blow, boys."

TERRIFIC TENNESSEE

44. Roy Acuff, "the King of Country Music" and Grand Ole Opry legend, was born Sept. 15, 1903, in Maynardsville. His most performed song was *The Wabash Cannonball*.

45. Seventeen different types of snails have been found in Snail Shell Cave near Murfreesboro. That's one cave with a slower pace.

46. Listen. The mockingbird was selected the state bird in 1933 by capturing 15,553 votes of 72,031 votes cast statewide. The robin came in a close second with 15,073 votes.

47. On Oct. 7, 1916, Lebanon's Cumberland University football squad suffered the sport's worst loss of all time when it was downed by Coach John Heisman's Georgia Tech team in Atlanta by a score of 222 to 0.

48. Back Valley's five-by-six-foot library is the smallest in America. The library door is never locked. Check it out.

TERRIFIC TENNESSEE

49. Chattanooga is home to the world's steepest incline railway, the Lookout Mountain Incline Railway, nicknamed "America's Most Amazing Mile" because of its 72.7% grade.

50. In 1924 Nashvillian John J. Harding Jr. was one of eight Army Air Service pilots who took part in the first flight around the world. They made the 27,000-mile trip in 15 days, three hours and seven minutes, averaging 72.5 miles per hour.

51. Grantland Rice, dean of American sports writers, was born in Murfreesboro on Nov. 1, 1880. In 1905 he became the first sports editor of *The Tennessean*. Remember, it's how you play the game that counts.

52. Would you believe that Tennessee trees that hold national records are a 110-foot-tall pin oak in Henderson County, a 107-foot-tall Fraser magnolia in Blount County and a 140-foot-tall red hickory in Sevier County? I wood.

TERRIFIC TENNESSEE

53. The Libertyland amusement park in Memphis boasts the oldest operating roller coaster in the United States with its Zippin Pippin, which was built there in 1915. Elvis used to rent the whole park for an evening to amuse his friends.

54. The nation's first major gold strike was in 1831 at Coker Creek. You can sift for gold there during the Autumn Gold Festival in October or any other time of the year.

55. The 10 most visited attractions in the state in 1995 were: (1) Dollywood, (2) Opryland, (3) The Tennessee Aquarium, (4) Ober Gatlinburg, (5) Gaylord Entertainment Performance Halls (Grand Ole Opry, Nashville on Stage and Ryman Auditorium), (6) Casey Jones Village, (7) Memphis Zoo & Aquarium, (8) Graceland, (9) Memphis Pink Palace Museum & Planetarium, (10) Rock City. See.

56. All roads lead to Fairview. It's the most common place name in the state with 26 towns or communities by that name.

TERRIFIC TENNESSEE

57. Singer-actress Dinah Shore was born in Winchester on March 1, 1917, and is well remembered for singing "See the U.S.A. in a Chevrolet" on her 1950s TV show, then throwing a kiss to the audience.

58. Tennessee (the state and the river) gets its name from Tanasi, the capital of the Cherokee Nation from 1721 to 1730. The name Tanasi was first recorded on a map in 1762 by Henry Timberlake. White men can't spell.

59. In 1874 Murfreesboro's Thankful Taylor, who had been suffering for five years with abdominal distress, had a 23-inch snake pulled from her mouth. Said Taylor, "Doctor, I feel like a great weight has been taken from my stomach."

60. Pomona's Margaret Bloodgood Peake began a philosophical cult which had a practice of letting young female members roll naked in clover moistened by the morning dew. The rite was abandoned when it was discovered the nearby woods were brimming with peeping Toms.

61. William Key's horse Jim Key of Shelbyville was known as the smartest horse in the world during the 1890s. The steed could recognize the letters of the alphabet, write his name with a piece of chalk and add and subtract numbers up to 25. Makes Mr. Ed look like a second grader, doesn't it.

62. The geographical center of the state is near Old Lascassas Pike, three miles north of the Murfreesboro public square. The spot is marked with a 26-foot obelisk.

63. Born in Covington on Aug. 20, 1942, Isaac Hayes won an Oscar and a Grammy for his theme for *Shaft*. Shut your mouth!

64. In the late 1940s and 1950s, Randy's Record Shop in Gallatin was America's largest mail-order record company. Owner Randy Wood also owned a record label, Dot Records, which launched the careers of such artists as Pat Boone, Billy Vaughan, Gale Storm, and the Hilltoppers.

TERRIFIC TENNESSEE

65. The only Tennessean to be knighted by royalty was Francis Joseph Campbell. Educated at the School for the Blind in Nashville in the 1840s, he established the Royal Normal School for the Blind in London and was knighted by King Edward VII.

66. Columbia native Dr. Marion Dorset, who developed a serum for hog cholera in 1910, was known as "the man who saved the swine industry." This actually means he saved our bacon.

67. Tennessee's largest cash crops are cotton, tobacco and soybeans. Memphis celebrates with its Memphis in May Festival, while Martin hosts a soybean festival in September.

68. At 11 A.M. each day at Memphis's Peabody Hotel, five ducks waddle to the sounds of John Philip Sousa's King Cotton March from their penthouse to the hotel lobby. Talk about animal quackers.

69. Hohenwald's Elephant Sanctuary offers refuge to Asian elephants and is now home to two pachyderms, with vacancies for 10 more. *Gilligan's Island* star Dawn Wells is celebrity spokeswoman.

70. When she died in the Maury County community of Lawrence in 1835, Aunt Betsy Trantham was reputedly 150 years old, which made her the oldest person to live on earth since biblical times and which also meant she lived during the 17th, 18th and 19th centuries.

71. The first Captain D's seafood restaurant was opened in Donelson in 1969. Today there are 600 restaurants.

72. Broadway and Metropolitan Opera Association star soprano Grace Moore, known as "the Tennessee Nightingale," was born near Del Rio on Dec. 5, 1901. At the zenith of her career in 1947, she died in an airplane accident.

TERRIFIC TENNESSEE

73. After Mary, a circus elephant, crushed her handler to death on Sept. 12, 1916, in Kingsport, 44,000 volts were zapped through her five-ton body with little effect. The next day she was hanged from a chain in Erwin until dead. Nobody remembers where she was buried, which is ironic considering an elephant never forgets.

74. Tennessean Sam Houston was the governor of both Tennessee and Texas and the president of the Republic of Texas, which proves Texans have good taste.

75. The lowest temperature recorded in Tennessee was 32 degrees below zero in Mountain City on Dec. 30, 1917, while the highest was 113 degrees in Perryville on Aug. 9, 1930.

76. Sequoyah, born at Tuskegee in Monroe County in 1776, completed an alphabet of 86 symbols for his Cherokee Nation in 1821. Sure would hate to have played him at Scrabble. The giant sequoia trees of California were named after him.

TERRIFIC TENNESSEE

77. The first children's lunch boxes with the image of a real-life person on the lid (a Hopalong Cassidy decal) were manufactured by Nashville's Aladdin Industries in 1951. They came in red or blue.

78. Railroad engineer Casey Jones, born Jonathan Luther Jones, was killed in a famous train wreck in Vaughan, Miss., on April 30, 1900. His home is now a museum in Jackson, where he was buried in Catholic Cemetery.

79. In 1877 Morristown preacher Melville M. Murrell invented a wing-flapping flying machine that he called the American Flying Machine. His ornithopter was not tested until 1911 when it was actually flown over 100 yards.

80. To this day a mystery hangs over the death of explorer Meriwether Lewis of Lewis and Clark fame: was it murder or suicide? In 1848 Tennessee erected a monument, a broken shaft, close to the site of his death near Hohenwald, symbolizing his premature death. It was made a national monument in 1925.

TERRIFIC TENNESSEE

81. Robert Taylor defeated his brother Alfred in "the War of the Roses" gubernatorial race of 1886. Robert wore a white rose to signify the Democratic Party, while Alfred wore a red rose for the Republican Party. Finally, in 1920 Alfred was elected governor. The boys were born and raised in Happy Valley. Figures.

82. Trenton's city hall houses the world's largest collection of antique teapots, 525 rare porcelain teapots made between 1750 and 1860 and shaped like people and animals.

83. Cornelia Fort, who was born in Nashville in 1919 and died in 1943, was America's first female pilot to die during service to her country. Cornelia Fort Airport in Nashville is named after her.

84. Mary Walker was born a slave and illiterate. But when she learned to read and write at the age of 117 in Chattanooga, the U.S. Department of Health, Education, and Welfare claimed her as the oldest student in the nation.

TERRIFIC TENNESSEE

85. Nashville is home to Thomas Nelson Company, the world's largest Bible publisher.

86. Moon Pies and RC Colas are the official snacks of Bell Buckle. In July 1995 Bell Buckle residents and guests devoured the world's largest Moon Pie.

87. It took a lot of nickels to build the Milky Way Farm outside Pulaski, but that's what candy magnate Frank C. Mars founded in 1932. During its heyday it was one of the top five farms in the nation. Now it is a country inn, corporate retreat, and honeymoon cottage. It has the largest dining table in the state, 14 baths, and 21 bedrooms.

88. Knoxville writer James Agee was highly regarded for his film reviews in *Time* and *Nation* during the 1940s. He later went to Hollywood and wrote screenplays (*The African Queen*). Agee won a Pulitzer Prize in 1958 for his novel *A Death in the Family*. It became a film in 1963 with Robert Preston portraying Agee's father and was shot on location in Knoxville.

89. The most bricks ever laid in one hour was 1,048 by Arlington's Sammy Wingfield on May 20, 1994. You sure can't say he was one shy of a load.

90. The highest point in the state is Clingman's Dome at 6,643 feet above sea level, while the lowest elevation is the Mississippi River in Shelby County at 182 feet.

91. Director Quentin Tarantino was born March 27, 1963, in Knoxville and named by his mom after the character Burt Reynolds played on *Gunsmoke*, blacksmith Quent Asper. The director's film credits include *Reservoir Dogs* and *Pulp Fiction*, the latter winning him an Oscar in 1995 for his scripting.

92. Uncle Dave Macon, "the Dixie Dew Drop" from Readyville, was the first major star of the Grand Ole Opry—singing, banjo-picking and grinning. Born in McMinnville, he loved to play *Bully of the Town* and *Chewin' Gum*.

93. Nat Love was born a slave in Davidson County in 1854 but became one of the most famous black cowboys of the American West because of his skills on horseback and working cattle drives. He earned the nickname "Deadwood Dick" after he captured first prize in a shooting, roping and riding contest in Deadwood, S.D. The cowboy wrote his autobiography, *The Life and Adventures of Nat Love, Better Known in the Cattle Country as Deadwood Dick*, in 1907.

94. When lots were auctioned off in Jackson in 1822, $20 worth of whiskey was passed around, compliments of the county court, to loosen the bidders' tongues. Doesn't anybody believe in traditions anymore?

95. John Rice Irwin has accumulated more than 250,000 artifacts to put together his Museum of Appalachia in Norris. It has been called "the most authentic and complete replica of pioneer Appalachian life in the world." Thanks a million, John.

TERRIFIC TENNESSEE

96. Nashville attorney Fred Thompson made his film debut playing himself in *Marie*. He later co-starred in *Cape Fear, The Hunt for Red October* and *In the Line of Fire*, before being elected U.S. Senator in 1994.

97. Nashville's Dr. Dorothy Brown was the first black woman to practice surgery in the South and the first to win election to the Tennessee General Assembly.

98. Oscar Robertson, nicknamed "the Big O," was born in Charlotte on Nov. 24, 1938, and was the second player in National Basketball Association history to score more than 25,000 points. A virtual scoring and passing machine from 1960 to 1974, the NBA's most valuable player of 1964 set an NBA career record of 9,887 assists.

99. Tiger Valley and Tiger Creek were named for James T. "Tiger" Whitehead, a Carter County hunter who killed 99 bears in his lifetime. The bears couldn't hold that Tiger.

TERRIFIC TENNESSEE

100. Swiss woodcarver Melchior Thoni settled in Nashville in 1869 and designed and carved the first wooden animals to stand on a merry-go-round.

101. Paris is the home of the world's largest fish fry each April when more than 10,000 pounds of catfish are consumed. Paris also has a 65-foot-high replica of the Eiffel Tower at the entrance of Memorial Park.

102. The quickest triplet birth on record was set by Mrs. James E. Duck of Memphis who gave natural birth to Bradley, Christopher and Carmon in two minutes on March 21, 1977.

103. Morgan Freeman was born June 1, 1937, in Memphis. Before he became a film star, in such movies as *Driving Miss Daisy, Unforgiven* and *Robin Hood: Prince of Thieves*, he played Easy Reader on PBS's *Electric Company*.

TERRIFIC TENNESSEE

104. The original MGM lion, Volney, lived at the Memphis Zoo and knew Johnny Weissmuller personally.

105. At 256 feet high, Fall Creek Falls is the highest waterfall east of the Mississippi.

106. Singing sensation Tennessee Ernie Ford was born Feb. 13, 1919, in Bristol. The great bass voice behind *Sixteen Tons* always ended his TV show with "Bless your little ol' pea-picking hearts."

107. The University of the South in Sewanee produces proportionately more Rhodes Scholars than any other school in the nation.

108. The great Hollywood director Walter Lang was born in Memphis on Aug. 10, 1898. Over a period of 35 years, his credits include *State Fair, Sentimental Journey, Cheaper by the Dozen, The King and I, Can-Can* and *Snow White and the Three Stooges.*

TERRIFIC TENNESSEE

109. Elizabethton's Doe River Covered Bridge, called the Kissing Bridge, is believed to be the oldest covered bridge in the state still in use. The 134-foot bridge was built of oak in 1882 and cost $3,000 to construct.

110. The Pemberton Oak or Royal Oak near South Holston Lake is estimated to be more than 700 years old. It gave shelter to soldiers of five wars: the Revolutionary War, the War of 1812, the Mexican War, the Civil War and World War I.

111. Film superstar Clint Eastwood sang on the stage of the Ryman Auditorium in 1982 while he was filming *Honky Tonk Man*.

112. The first newspaper in the U.S. devoted entirely to freeing slaves, the *Manumission Intelligencer* (later renamed the *Emancipator*), was established in Jonesborough in 1819 by Elihu Embree.

TERRIFIC TENNESSEE

113. In 1842 the first railroad in the state was the Memphis and La Grange with six miles of track. By 1861 there were 1,200 miles of railroad lines in the state but the Memphis and La Grange had folded.

114. University of Tennessee football star Reggie White makes tackles for the Green Bay Packers and during the off-season says his prayers as an associate minister for the Inner City Church in Knoxville.

115. In the early 1900s, well before TVA was born, Cannon County's Readyville Mill offered local homeowners electricity for 50 cents a month. At one time, mill operator "Rat" McFerrin had a lever hooked up to his henhouse which turned the electricity off and on in the mornings and evenings by the weight of his chickens getting in and out of their nests.

116. In 1913 Knoxville became the only city in the world with mailboxes on its city buses and streetcars.

117. H. Jackson Brown's *Life's Little Instruction Book* has sold more than 10 million copies in 20 different languages, in 26 countries since 1991. The Nashvillian gives good advice.

118. Ornithologists have spotted 316 different types of birds in the state.

119. Nashville's Meharry Medical College, begun in 1876, was the nation's first all-black medical school. About 40% of all black physicians and dentists practicing in the U.S. are Meharry grads.

120. The first concrete highway in the state was built in 1921 and extended 14 miles from Athens to the Hiawassee River at Calhoun. That was a long hard road.

121. Tennesseans cast more than 145,000 votes in the presidential race of 1860. The winner, Abraham Lincoln, received not a single vote from the state.

TERRIFIC TENNESSEE

122. There are 1,405 state historical markers across Tennessee, and it costs about $1,240 to have one erected.

123. The first steamboat to reach Nashville (March 11, 1819) on the Cumberland River was the *General Jackson*, the same name of the showboat operated today by Opryland. The first steamboat to navigate the entire length of the Tennessee River was the *Atlas* in 1828. The captain captured a prize of $650 from the city of Knoxville.

124. One of the founders of the Lafayette Escadrille of the French Army Aviation Corps was Newport's Kiffin Yates Rockwell. In July 1916 he was involved in more air battles than any other pilot in French aviation. He was killed that year in a battle with a German pilot and was awarded the Legion of Honor and the Croix de Guerre.

125. The Dempster Dumpster was invented by Will Dempster in Knoxville in 1933.

TERRIFIC TENNESSEE

126. Russell's Popcorn Company in Hartsville makes its popcorn on the third floor of a Methodist church that was erected in 1850. The family has been popping since 1925 and the company motto is "Grown in sunshine, popped in moonshine."

127. The Knoxville World's Fair of 1982 attracted 11 million visitors who went Tenne-seein'.

128. There are four mountains near Townsend named Matthew, Mark, Luke and John. And that's the gospel truth.

129. In 1904 William Haskell Neal of Tuckers Crossroads in Wilson County developed Neal's Paymaster Corn, the first stalks of corn to have more than one ear of corn per stalk. Did that make him a corny stalker?

130. A world-leading 27 species of salamanders have been seen in the Great Smoky Mountain National Park, making it "the Salamander Capitol of the U.S."

TERRIFIC TENNESSEE

131. Rock and film star Tina Turner was born Annie Mae Bullock on Nov. 26, 1938, in Nutbush and began her singing career in the choir of Brownsville's Spring Hill Baptist Church.

132. Tennessean Almeron Dickenson was in charge of the artillery at the Alamo. His wife, Susannah Wilkinson Dickenson, survived the battle and was thereafter known as "the Lady of the Alamo."

133. Ebbing and Flowing Spring, three miles east of Rogersville, presents a natural phenomenon where the water ebbs to a low point and then revives rapidly in about 10 minutes until it reaches its zenith nearly two and a half hours later. This cycle has been repeated for at least 200 years.

134. The oldest known song about the state is *Ellie Rhee*, later named *Carry Me Back to Tennessee*, which was written by Septimus Winner in 1865.

TERRIFIC TENNESSEE

135. The University of Tennessee's football stadium, which seats more fans (107,000+) than any other outdoor stadium in the U.S., is named after Gen. Robert R. Neyland, the legendary Vol coach who won 171 games, lost 31 and had 12 ties.

136. One of the earliest Gatling Guns was constructed in a blacksmith shop near the Sinking Creek Baptist Church in 1864 by Robert and Cann Peoples and is buried near the church building.

137. The state reptile is the Eastern box turtle. Let 'em cross the road, please.

138. Former *Tennessean* newspaperboy James Craig, who bore a strong resemblance to Clark Gable, was born in Nashville on Feb. 4, 1912, and starred in the films *The Devil and Daniel Webster, Kitty Foyle, The Human Comedy, Our Vines Have Tender Grapes* and *All That Money Can Buy*.

TERRIFIC TENNESSEE

139. Brownsville boasts a collection of Abraham Lincoln books and memorabilia in its Lincoln Museum.

140. Cowboy great Tex Ritter ran for the Republican nomination for a U.S. Senate seat from Tennessee in 1970 and lost. Still, we do not forsake him.

141. The original name of Erwin was Vanderbilt. It was renamed to honor the town physician, Dr. J.N. Ervin, but the U.S. Post Office accidentally spelled it Erwin.

142. Danny Thomas founded St. Jude's Hospital in Memphis in 1958 as the result of a prayer to St. Jude, the patron saint of the helpless, when he asked for a sign that his career in show biz would succeed.

143. During the 1960s and 1970s Memphis's Stax Records was the record label of such musical greats as Booker T & the MG's, Issac Hayes, Otis Redding and Sam and Dave.

TERRIFIC TENNESSEE

144. Memphian Cary Middlecoff, a member of the Professional Golf Association Hall of Fame, was the leading money winner on the PGA tour during the 1950s and has captured 39 PGA tour events.

145. The picture of the young girl on Martha White Flour packages is that of Martha White Lindsey, born in 1899, whose father, Richard Lindsey, owned the Royal Flour Mill of Nashville.

146. The Andy Griffith Show Rerun Watchers Club was founded in 1979 on the campus of Vanderbilt University. Today there are more than 20,000 members in over 40 states. For info, send a self-addressed stamped envelope to TAGSRWC, 9 Music Square South, Suite 146, Nashville, TN 37203-3203. You'll be glad you did.

147. Aretha Franklin, "the godmother of soul," was born the daughter of a Baptist preacher on March, 25, 1942, in Memphis.

TERRIFIC TENNESSEE

148. Gen. Nathan Bedford Forrest, born in Chapel Hill on July 13, 1821, led the way the only time a cavalry defeated a naval force. His philosophy: "Get there first with the most men." The brilliant tactician entered the Civil War as a private.

149. The oldest wild cranberry bogs in the U.S. are in Shady Valley in Johnson County. Only one-tenth of an acre remains of bogs that covered 10,000 acres in 1857. Shady Valley hosts a cranberry festival in October.

150. Notorious outlaw of the Natchez Trace John Murrell, who was born in Williamson County in 1804, died of tuberculosis in Pikeville in 1844, after serving a prison term for stealing slaves.

151. *I Walk the Line*, which was filmed near Cookeville in 1970 and starred Gregory Peck and Tuesday Weld, was based on Tennessee author Madison Jones's novel *An Exile*. The theme song was sung by Johnny Cash.

TERRIFIC TENNESSEE

152. Fisk University's Jubilee Hall was the nation's first permanent building used exclusively for the education of blacks. When the school nearly went bankrupt, the Jubilee Singers began touring (1871) to raise funds and became so famous as singers of spirituals that Queen Victoria had their portrait commissioned.

153. Tennessee's Centennial Exposition of 1897 was officially opened from Washington, D.C., when President McKinley pushed a button that fired a cannon in Nashville.

154. Surprise! The first Holiday Inn was built in Memphis in 1952.

155. Tennessee towns that host pumpkin festivals include Fayetteville, Allardt and Franklin. Allardt is the official Southeastern weigh-in location for pumpkins.

156. Jim Bowie, famous for his big knife, was born at Station Camp Creek in Sumner County in 1796.

157. The first American soldier killed in the Vietnam War was Tom Davis of Livingston, on Dec. 22, 1961, his 25th birthday.

158. Harvesting half a million pearls annually, the American Pearl Farm in Camden is the only successful pearl-culturing operation in the U.S. Its owner, John Latendresse, has the largest collection of freshwater pearls in the world.

159. Shot in Nashville in 1965, *Second Fiddle to a Steel Guitar* may have featured more country music stars than any other film. In the cast were Kitty Wells, Webb Pierce, Lefty Frizzell, Carl & Pearl Butler, Bill Monroe, Del Reeves, George Hamilton IV, Faron Young, Minnie Pearl, Sonny James, Little Jimmy Dickens, Johnny Wright, Dottie West, Merle Kilgore, Billy Walker, Pete Drake, Connie Smith, Homer & Jethro, Arnold Stang and two of the Bowery Boys, Huntz Hall and Leo Gorcey.

TERRIFIC TENNESSEE

160. The Tennessee Walking Horse is the only breed to be named for a state. The first grand champion was Strolling Jim of Wartrace, who is buried behind the town's Walking Horse Hotel.

161. Germantown's Ted Shuler has a world record 3,080 full bottles of different varieties of beer. Take one down and pass it around.

162. Dale Hollow Lake is home to the world's only freshwater jellyfish.

163. The first dogs trained to guide blind people were schooled by the Seeing Eye organization in Nashville in 1929. Morris Frank and his German shepherd, Buddy, were the first team in America to break the barrier. The Disney TV movie *Love Leads the Way*, about Morris and Buddy, was filmed in Franklin in 1984 with Timothy Bottoms as Morris Frank.

164. Baptists are the largest religious group in the state.

165. Smyrna's Sam Davis was "the Boy Hero of the Confederacy" who at age 21 was hanged as a spy on Nov. 27, 1863. "If I had a thousand lives, I would lose them all here and now before I would betray my friends,'' Davis said. There is a statue of him on the Pulaski square and a museum on the spot where he was hanged.

166. At 1,120 feet below the surface of Lookout Mountain, Ruby Falls is the deepest cavern in the U.S. and boasts the highest underground waterfall open to the public. The 145-foot underground waterfall was named after Ruby Losey, the first woman to see it. Hmm, Losey Falls? Naah.

167. "The Tennessee Plowboy," Eddy Arnold, was born in Henderson on May 15, 1918. The velvet-voiced singer has sold over 85 million records.

168. Jack Daniel's Distillery is the oldest registered distillery in the nation. Old Jack had a bad temper and died from gangrene after kicking an iron stove in his office.

169. Memphis native Anfernee "Penny" Hardaway of the National Basketball Association's Orlando Magic has a tattoo of a bulldog with the number 1 on his left leg, representing his jersey number.

170. It was Teddy Roosevelt, after a visit to Nashville's Maxwell House hotel, who pronounced about its java, "Good to the last drop."

171. Homer & Jethro of country comedy fame were Henry D. Haynes (Homer), born March 10, 1923, in Knoxville and Kenneth C. Burns (Jethro), born July 29, 1917, in Knoxville. They won a Grammy in 1959 and were well known in the 1960s for their Kellogg's Cornflake commercials. One of their biggest hits was *The Battle of Kookamonga*.

172. The first American horse to win the English Derby was Iroquois, bred at Nashville's Belle Meade Plantation in 1881. When one of the plantation's famous horses, Enquirer, died in 1895, the *Cincinnati Enquirer*, which shared the horse's name, sent 300 mourners to the funeral.

173. Blue Springs Cave, mapped up to 33 miles, is the longest cave in the state, while McMinnville's Cumberland Caverns has the largest cave room in eastern America and boasts a one-ton crystal chandelier in its Volcano Room.

174. Representatives of every species of duck on the Mississippi Flyway can be found in the Dr. Walter E. David Wildife Museum at Dyersburg State Community College. It's all that it's quacked up to be.

175. Contemporary Christian and pop singer Amy Grant, whose voice provided the hits *Baby Baby, Every Heartbeat* and *House of Love*, grew up in Nashville and is an alumna of Belmont University.

TERRIFIC TENNESSEE

176. There are 36 natural bridges in Tennessee. Take that, Madison County.

177. The Tennessee Valley Authority was created by Congress on May 18, 1933. Between 1933 and 1951, the TVA built 20 hydroelectric dams and purchased or condemned 1.1 million acres, of which 300,000 acres were flooded.

178. Vice President Al Gore was raised in Carthage and Washington, D.C., and met wife-to-be, Tipper (Mary Elizabeth Aitcheson), when they were both high school students. He was 17 and she was 16. They married May 19, 1970, to the sounds of *All You Need Is Love*, and their first home was in a trailer park in Daleville, Alabama.

179. The only museum in the nation dedicated solely to the art and craft of fine metalwork is the National Ornamental Metal Museum in Memphis. Steel yourself for a treat.

TERRIFIC TENNESSEE

180. Bessie Smith, "Empress of the Blues," was born in Chattanooga in 1894 and began her singing career on the streets of Chattanooga. Just one month after the release of her *Down Hearted Blues* in 1923, more than 750,000 copies were sold. The sole visual recording of her vocalizing is in the short film *St. Louis Blues*.

181. The Memphis site of the assassination of Dr. Martin Luther King Jr., the former Lorraine Motel, is now the National Civil Rights Museum.

182. The oldest working family-owned general store in the Mid-South is A. Schwab's on Beale Street in Memphis. Begun in 1876, the store's motto is "If you can't find it at A. Schwab's, then you are better off without it!"

183. Cordell Hull, "the Father of the United Nations," was born Oct. 2, 1871, in a log cabin near Byrdstown and won the Nobel Peace Prize in 1945. He served as U.S. secretary of state longer than anyone else.

184. Davidson County's Mark Robertson Cockrill was known as the wool king of the world in 1851 when his fleece captured the top prize at the London Crystal Palace Exposition. He was itching to win.

185. During the Civil War battle of Mobile Bay it was Knoxville native Adm. David Glasgow Farragut who uttered the immortal words, "Damn the torpedoes! Full speed ahead!" Congress created the rank of full admiral for him in 1866.

186. One of the first films to be shot in the state was *The Bishop of Cottontown* in 1928. The silent film, which re-created the battle of Franklin, was never finished, but for two days, hundreds of extras dressed as Civil War soldiers had a great time pretending to be at war.

187. Written by Tennessee native Wallace Saunders, an African-American fireman who rode with Jones, *The Ballad of Casey Jones* is considered the most popular folk ballad in American history.

TERRIFIC TENNESSEE

188. The state insects are the ladybug and the firefly (or lightnin' bug).

189. Nashville swimmer Tracy Caulkins brought home four gold medals from the 1984 Olympics. She set five world records and won 48 national titles during her career.

190. It was Tennessee's ratification that put the 19th Amendment in the Constitution giving women the right to vote.

191. Bradford is "the Doodle Soup Capital of the World." You can have a free bowl the fourth week of July. The soup is made of chicken drippings with hot pepper and vinegar and is best eaten drizzled over crackers, biscuits or bread. Umm, umm.

192. Fred Smith founded Federal Express in Memphis in 1973. The first night of business, the company shipped 18 packages. On a recent Christmas Eve, FedEx shipped over two million packages in a single day.

TERRIFIC TENNESSEE

193. Interred in the Nashville City Cemetery is Capt. William Driver, the man who nicknamed the flag "Old Glory." A flag is flown day and night there in his honor.

194. Home of the National Association for the Preservation and Perpetuation of Storytelling, Jonesborough hosts the National Storytelling Festival each October. No lie.

195. The Shiloh Motor Hotel in Seymour is the only biker hotel in the U.S. You gotta be driving a motorcycle to get a room, dig?

196. The first recording of country music was by Ralph Peer in Bristol on Aug. 1, 1927 when he recorded A.P., Sara and Maybelle Carter's renditions of *The Poor Orphan Child* and *Bury Me Under the Weeping Willow*. A few days later Jimmie Rodgers recorded *The Soldier's Sweetheart* and *Sleep, Baby, Sleep*. The Bristol recording sessions for Victor became the first country records distributed nationally.

TERRIFIC TENNESSEE

197. James K. Polk, eleventh president of the U.S., was so close to Andrew Jackson that he was nicknamed "Young Hickory." His wife, Sarah Childress, allowed no card playing, dancing or alcoholic beverages in the White House. Polk is buried on the grounds of the state capitol, while his family's ancestral home is always open to visitors in Columbia.

198. The first Catholic church in the state, Holy Rosary Cathedral, was built in Nashville in 1820. The first Jewish congregation in the state was established in Nashville in 1848.

199. Gainesboro hosts an annual Poke Sallet Festival the first week of May, which has no connection to the song *Poke Sallet Annie*, written by Nashville songwriter Tony Joe White, other than the chomp, chomp, chomping going on.

200. Nashville Vol slugger Bob Lennon smashed 64 home runs in 1954.

TERRIFIC TENNESSEE

201. The July heat in 1925 chased the folks involved in Dayton's Scopes Monkey Trial from the courthouse and into the outdoors as William Jennings Bryan and Clarence Darrow argued the case of evolution as fact or fantasy for eight days. Robinson's Drugstore did a brisk business serving Monkey Fizzes.

202. The first European to enter what was to become Tennessee was Hernando De Soto in 1540.

203. Country music comedian Archie Campbell of *Hee Haw* fame was born in Bulls Gap on Nov. 17, 1914.

204. Oak Ridge was nicknamed "Atomic City" and "the Energy Capital of the World" because of the huge Manhattan Project which employed 13,000 workers in 1943 as scientists developed the atom bomb. It cost $96 million to build the town. To keep things as secret as possible, 90 square miles of land were fenced in with only seven entrance gates.

TERRIFIC TENNESSEE

205. Tennessee's first geologist, Dr. Gerald Troost, mapped the state for geological reasons and around 1831 estimated he had walked 10,000 miles criss-crossing the state. However, he wore no checkered shirt.

206. The world's largest underground lake, 4.5 acres wide and 140 feet below the surface, is the Lost Sea in Sweetwater's Craighead Caverns.

207. During the Civil War 187,000 Tennesseans joined the Confederate army, while 51,000 fought for the Federal side. This means that Tennessee contributed more soldiers than any other state.

208. Knoxville gets "bugged" each August during its Volunteer Bug Jam. There are tons of Bugs but no insects; the Bugs are VWs.

209. Columbia is well known as "the Mule Capital of the World" and hosts a Mule Day in April, which draws 50,000 to 70,000 people.

TERRIFIC TENNESSEE

210. In 1921 Tennessean Ann Lee Worley was the first woman in the U.S. to be elected to a state senate position.

211. Rugby was the last organized English colony in the U.S. The community's Thomas Hughes Free Public Library contains the greatest collection of Victorian literature in the nation.

212. Robert Church Sr. is said to have been the first black millionaire in the South. The Memphian bought land on Beale Street in 1899 and built an auditorium and park, creating America's first cultural center for African Americans.

213. Claude Jarman Jr., who was born Sept. 27, 1934, in Nashville, won a special Academy Award as a child when he played the son of Gregory Peck and Jane Wyman in *The Yearling* (1946). He also starred in *Intruder in the Dust* and *Rio Grande*.

TERRIFIC TENNESSEE

214. Jessica Lange went country when she starred as Patsy Cline in *Sweet Dreams*, the 1984 film shot in Nashville.

215. The first professional team that Baseball Hall of Famer Willie Mays played for was the Chattanooga Choo Choos in the summer of 1947. Mays was 16. Say hey!

216. In June 1957 Clinton's Bobby Cain became the first African American to graduate from an integrated public high school in the South.

217. The Grand Guitar Museum outside of Bristol is reportedly the only building in the world shaped like a guitar. It's easy to pick out. Unfortunately, it is now closed.

218. Astronaut Rhea Seddon, who was born in Murfreesboro on Sept. 8, 1947, was one of the first six women in space. The former Murfreesboro Central High School cheerleader spent a seven-day flight in the space shuttle *Discovery*.

TERRIFIC TENNESSEE

219. The first theatrical performance given in Nashville occurred Dec. 4, 1807, with a double bill: a drama, *The Child of Nature, or Virtue Rewarded*, and a farce, *The Purse or the Benevolent Tar*.

220. Using a rowboat, Memphian Tom Lee saved 32 people's lives on May 8, 1925, after an excursion boat capsized on the Mississippi River. Lee couldn't swim.

221. Between 1917 and 1957, Southern Potteries, Inc., of Erwin produced more than 24 million pieces of Blue Ridge Pottery, a record that may be hard to break.

222. Country music singer-songwriter Rosanne Cash was born May 24, 1955, in Memphis.

223. Tennessee is No. 1 in the nation in the production of aluminum. And that's "Alrighta with Alcoa," where in 1910 the Aluminum Company of America set up shop on the Little Tennessee River.

224. The Cloudland Hotel, built by Gen. John T. Wilder in 1877 astride Roan Mountain, boasted that guests could sleep in Tennessee and eat in North Carolina without leaving the same building. The banquet table had a white stripe down the middle with "Tennessee" painted on one side and "North Carolina" on the other.

225. The first all-African-American radio station was Memphis's WDIA, in 1948.

226. Frances Hodgson Burnett, the British-born author of such novels as *Little Lord Fauntleroy* and *The Secret Garden*, lived in New Market as a teenager in 1865 and later moved to Knoxville.

227. The Highlander Folk School in New Market was originally started in Monteagle in 1932 by Myles Horton to promote a progressive labor movement. It was at Highlander that *We Shall Overcome* originated as the anthem of the civil rights movement.

TERRIFIC TENNESSEE

228. Roan Mountain State Park boasts one of the world's largest stand of Catawba rhododendron bushes, 600 acres of 'em. Talk about the color purple, you should see 'em bloom in June.

229. Rocky Mount, the oldest original territorial capitol still standing on its original site (1770), was the first capitol of present-day Tennessee and the first territorial capitol west of the Alleghenies.

230. Cookeville's Wilson Sporting Goods made every New York Yankee uniform that Mickey Mantle ever wore. They must have made a good pitch.

231. Chickamauga and Chattanooga National Military Park is the nation's oldest, largest and most visited military park.

232. Tennessee's oldest courthouse is in Charlotte, county seat of Dickson County. Built in 1833, the original building was encased in brick in 1930 to match new wings to the structure.

TERRIFIC TENNESSEE

233. Limestone's Moody Dunbar Pepper Plant processes as much as 250 tons of pepper and pimientos daily, making it the largest pepper and pimiento production plant in the world.

234. Host of the game show *Tic Tac Dough* and the hit singer of *Deck of Cards*, Wink Martindale was born in Jackson on Dec. 4, 1934.

235. Julia Doak was the first woman to hold the office of state superintendent of education in the U.S.

236. A wagon road from Knoxville to Nashville was completed in 1795. However, they're still working on a portion of it in Knoxville.

237. Lafayette's Nera White, a 13-time Amateur Athletics' Union All-American, was one of the first two women inducted into the National Basketball Hall of Fame in 1992. She was an AAU All-American 15 years.

TERRIFIC TENNESSEE

238. Pringles Potato Chips are made in Jackson by Snoco.

239. William Bean was the first permanent resident of Tennessee when he constructed a log cabin beside the Watauga River in 1769. His son, Russell, was the first white child born in Tennessee.

240. Reelfoot Lake, the state's only major natural lake, was created by the New Madrid earthquake of 1811-1812 when the Mississippi River flowed backward. Its 13,000 acres provide habitat for many animals, fish and birds, including the bald eagle.

241. Andrew Jackson, seventh president of the U.S., was nicknamed Old Hickory because of his toughness. He engaged in duels, loved horse racing and cockfighting and was a champion soldier at battling Indians and the British. His Nashville home, the Hermitage, is a national shrine and is filled with more original furnishings than any other presidential home in the U.S.

TERRIFIC TENNESSEE

242. Tennessean Melanie Smith was the first woman to win the American Gold Cup, the richest horse-jumping contest in the world.

243. When it opened in Clarksville on Oct. 6, 1919, the First Women's Bank of Tennessee was the nation's first bank totally organized and operated by women.

244. Carl Perkins of *Blue Suede Shoes* fame was born April 19, 1932, in Tiptonville. He has a restaurant in Jackson. Step on in sometime.

245. The state animal is the raccoon.

246. *The Knoxville Gazette* was the first newspaper in the state when James Miller began publishing it on Nov. 5, 1791, in Rogersville.

247. Tupperware is made in Halls, thus Tupperware hails from Halls. Let's party.

248. Nancy Ward, "Beloved Woman" of the Cherokees, who was known as "the Pocahontas of Tennessee," was born in July 1740 at Chota, capital of the Cherokee Nation. She fought beside braves against Indian enemies and helped save the lives of many white settlers.

249. Sinking Creek Baptist Church, built in 1803 between Elizabethton and Johnson City, is the oldest church in the state.

250. Actor John Cullum of TV's *Northern Exposure* was born in Knoxville on March 2, 1930. The winner of two best actor Tony Awards (*Shenandoah* in 1975 and *On the Twentieth Century* in 1978), he made his Broadway debut in *Camelot* as Sir Dinadan and was also a stand-in for Richard Burton.

251. The battle of Shiloh, April 6-7, 1862, was one of the bloodiest of the Civil War as 23,746 men died in battle. It was the first western battle of the Civil War.

TERRIFIC TENNESSEE

252. The general office building of General Shale Products Corporation in Johnson City has 16 sides inscribed within a 100-foot circle. It is also home to General Shale's Museum of Ancient Brick. Ernest T. Bass's idea of heaven, I suppose.

253. Kitty Wells, "the Queen of Country Music," was born Muriel Deason in Nashville on Aug. 13, 1919. It wasn't God who made honky-tonk angels, but He sure gave Kitty a heavenly voice.

254. The state gem is the Tennessee River pearl. The state's pearl industry is a $20 to $60 million annual business.

255. President's Island near Memphis is the largest island in the Mississippi River. Originally named Jackson Island after President Jackson, it consists of 32,000 acres.

256. The world's highest-banked international stock car raceway is the Bristol International Raceway.

TERRIFIC TENNESSEE

257. Jesse James, under the alias of John Davis Howard, lived with his wife and son in Denver, Humphreys County, in the late 1870s. His son, Jesse Edwards, was born in Nashville in 1875, and the twins, Monty and Gould, who died at birth in 1878, are buried in Denver.

258. Only one Tennessee county is named after a woman. Grainger County honors Mary Grainger Blount, the wife of territorial governor William Blount.

259. The first school in the state was begun by Rev. Samuel Doak in 1780 near Jonesborough. It eventually evolved into the oldest educational institution in the state, Washington College. Doak, a Presbyterian, was also the first minister to live in the state.

260. Nashville's Citizens Bank is the oldest continuously operating African-American-owned bank in the U.S. It opened in 1904 as the One Cent Savings Bank.

TERRIFIC TENNESSEE

261. Oscar-winner Kathy Bates, for *Misery* (1990), was born June 28, 1948, in Memphis. Her other films include *Fried Green Tomatoes, Dick Tracy* and *Come Back to the Five and Dime Jimmy Dean Jimmy Dean.*

262. Kenton is one of only four towns in the U.S. that is the home of white squirrels.

263. Check out the Sears & Roebuck house at 518 Cumberland Street in Cowan. It was ordered from the catalog in the early 1900s. There is also a Sears house in Pulaski at 417 West Jefferson, built around 1915.

264. Shelbyville has been nicknamed "Pencil City" because of its pencil-making industry. They can really get the lead out.

265. Worth Inc. in Tullahoma is the world's largest manufacturer of bats and baseballs, producing one million bats and seven million balls per year. Let's play two.

266. They've been battling with hard-boiled eggs in Peters Hollow near Elizabethton every Easter since 1823. Some Peters Hollow egg fights have drawn more than 1,000 contestants with over 7,000 eggs.

267. Over the years Nashville's historic Ryman Auditorium hosted not only country music legends, but a number of stars from other fields, including Booker T. Washington, Sarah Bernhardt, Robert Peary, Helen Keller, Charlie Chaplin, Enrico Caruso, Isadora Duncan, Rudolph Valentino, Will Rogers, Fanny Brice, Basil Rathbone, Orson Welles, Helen Hayes, Nelson Eddy, Jeanette MacDonald, Katharine Hepburn, Bela Lugosi, Bob Hope, Doris Day, Harpo Marx, Roy Rogers, Mae West and Gene Autry.

268. Three ferries still operate in the state: Clifton Ferry in Wayne County, Saltillo Ferry in Hardin County, and the Cumberland City Ferry in Stewart County. This is no ferry tale.

TERRIFIC TENNESSEE

269. Memphis mechanic P.J. "Pete" Lunati invented the compressed air and hydraulic car lift in 1925, which sure made changing your oil a lot easier.

270. Come Christmastime, Elizabethton has the world's tallest decorated Fraser fir tree. At other seasons, it's the world's second tallest Fraser fir.

271. In 1980 Jane Eskind became the first woman to win a statewide election when she was elected to the Public Service Commission.

272. White House's Jim Varney has established himself as quite an earnest actor in Tennessee. He made four "Ernest" films in the state, including *Ernest Goes to Camp* (1986), *Ernest Saves Christmas* (1988), *Ernest Goes to Jail* (1989) and *Ernest Scared Stupid* (1991).

273. Elvis Presley's Graceland is the second-most-visited house in the U.S., behind only the White House.

TERRIFIC TENNESSEE

274. Camp Tyson near Paris was the site of the nation's only barrage balloon base, where from 1941 to 1944 several thousand soldiers were trained to deploy tethered balloons to a height of about one mile to present an obstacle to bomber pilots.

275. National Football League star Claude Humphrey was born in Memphis on June 29, 1944, played for Tennessee State University and was the NFL defensive rookie of the year in 1968 for the Atlanta Falcons. We applaud Claude.

276. An Ooltewah family business, Litespeed, made all or part of the bicycles ridden by the U.S. Road and Team Trial Racing Cycling team during the 1996 Olympics. The company also supplied parts to racing teams from Belgium, England, France, Mexico and Poland.

277. Arnold Engineering Development Center in Tullahoma is the largest aerodynamic testing facility in the world.

TERRIFIC TENNESSEE

278. In October Henderson County is home to the Possum Festival in the Parkers Crossroads community, complete with "the world's largest possum hunt" and possum races. Everything is possumable.

279. Perhaps the most famous country honky tonk of them all is Tootsie's Orchid Lounge on Nashville's Lower Broadway. In 1960 the owner, Hattie Louise Bess, painted the joint purple and opened for business.

280. The Nashville Network went on the air on March 7, 1983. The first show was *Launch Night*, hosted by Ralph Emery, which soon became *Nashville Now*. The first performer was Con Hunley. Today, TNN goes into 69 million homes around the world.

281. DeFord Bailey was the first African American to perform on the Grand Ole Opry when he blew into his harmonica in 1926. Dubbed "the Wizard of the Harmonica," he was born in the Bellwood community near the Smith-Wilson County line in 1899.

TERRIFIC TENNESSEE

282. The state's first radio station was WOAN, begun in Lawrenceburg by James D. Vaughn on Nov. 21, 1922. The first TV station was WMC-TV in Memphis, which went on the air on Dec. 11, 1948.

283. Built in 1852, the Cumberland Tunnel near Cowan is the nation's largest and steepest railroad tunnel. It's 2,200 feet long, 21 feet high and 15 feet wide.

284. Chattanooga's Estes Kefauver ran for the U.S. Senate while politicking in a coonskin cap in 1948 and won. In 1956 he was the Democratic vice presidential nominee alongside Adlai Stevenson.

285. The oldest survivor of the Civil War was the Confederate Army's John B. Salling, who died at age 113 on March 16, 1959, in Kingsport.

286. Pipe down and visit the Museum of Tobacco Art & History in Nashville, which features a quilt (circa 1880) made from 500 silk cigar ribbons. Admission is free.

TERRIFIC TENNESSEE

287. A company in Philadelphia bought the entire town of Norris for $2.1 million in 1948 and then resold the place in lots. Wonder who got Park Place and Boardwalk?

288. The United Daughters of the Confederacy was organized in Nashville in 1894 by Caroline Meriwether Goodlett.

289. Two character actor greats made tracks from Tennessee to Hollywood: Bill McKinney of Chattanooga (*Deliverance, Bronco Billy, The Outlaw Josey Wales*) and William Sanderson of Memphis (*Newhart, Lonesome Dove, Blade Runner*).

290. Stuntman-turned-director Hal Needham was born in Memphis on March 6, 1934. His movie credits include *The War Wagon, Little Big Man, Semi-Tough* and *Hooper*.

291. The choo choo first entered Chattanooga on Dec. 1, 1849. Today a railroad museum is there.

TERRIFIC TENNESSEE

292. Oprah Winfrey grew up in Nashville, where her father was a barber, and graduated from East High School and Tennessee State University. The talk show host was a news reporter for WTVF long before she became one of the richest women in the U.S. She was also the first Miss Black Tennessee. Her production company is named Harpo, which is Oprah spelled backwards.

293. The motorized cotton picker was invented in 1928 by brothers John D. and Mack D. Rust of Memphis. It was a cotton-picking blessing.

294. Du Pont built the world's largest smokeless gunpowder plant in Old Hickory in 1918. In a matter of several weeks, the community grew from 12 families to 100,000 people. The place was dyno-mite!

295. Dallas Cowboys football star "Too Tall" Jones was born Feb. 23, 1951, in Jackson. The defensive end never missed a game except for the 1979 season when he was a pro boxer. The big guy played in three Super Bowls.

TERRIFIC TENNESSEE

296. Weakley County produces more sweet potato slips than any other place in the U.S. Thus the town of Gleason is nicknamed "Tatertown."

297. The four different mineral waters (red, white, black, and double and twist) of Red Boiling Springs are good for what ails you, or so the story goes. The town hosts a Folk Medicine Festival each July, so go drink up.

298. *What Waits Below* or *Secrets of the Phantom Caverns* was filmed in Cumberland Caverns in 1983 and starred British actor Robert Powell, who portrayed Christ in *Jesus of Nazareth*.

299. During the 1970s the U.S. Post Office in Hornbeak had an official stamp licker in Rex the mongrel. Rex normally licked off a roll of 100 stamps at a time.

300. Memphis is the second largest inland port in the United States.

TERRIFIC TENNESSEE

301. The earliest known quilt made in Tennessee was pieced by Rebecca Foster in 1808. It is now on display in the Tennessee State Museum in Nashville.

302. George Hamilton was born Aug. 12, 1939, in Memphis. The guy with a great tan starred in the films *Where the Boys Are, Evel Knievel, Love at First Bite* and *Zorro, the Gay Blade.*

303. Chet Akins, known as "Mr. Guitar" and one of the those most responsible for making Nashville "Music City," was born June 20, 1924, in Luttrell.

304. One of the most famous haunted spots in the nation is the Bell Witch Cave near Adams, where the ghost of Kate Batts first appeared in 1817. It was reported to have even spooked Andrew Jackson.

305. The Flyaway in Pigeon Forge is a vertical wind tunnel that simulates skydiving indoors and is the only one in the U.S. Geronimo!

TERRIFIC TENNESSEE

306. The youngest senator in the history of Congress was Tennessee Democrat John Henry Eaton, who was sworn in on Nov. 16, 1818, when he was a tender 28 years, 4 months and 29 days old.

307. From the 1940s through the 1960s there were over 800 barns in 19 states that carried the message "See Rock City." Most of them were painted by Clark Byers.

308. Director Robert Altman's *Nashville* is considered by some film critics to be the finest movie of the 1970s. Shot on location in and around Music City, the film was a mosaic of American life looking at 24 characters at a political rally.

309. The most golf played in one week was 1,128 holes by Steve Hylton on Clarksville's Mason Rudolph Golf Course, Aug. 25-31, 1980.

310. The nation's first African-American federal judge was Knoxville's William H. Hastie.

TERRIFIC TENNESSEE

311. *Time Magazine* has stated that the ice cream from Athens's Mayfield Dairy Farms is "one of the best in the world." That's a cold soft fact.

312. The state flower is the iris, while the state wildflower is the passion flower.

313. The first public library in the state was opened in Nashville in 1813.

314. Norris Lake claims to be "the Rockfish Capital of the World," while Mount Juliet is known as "the Purple Martin Capital of the World."

315. Frank Sutton, famous as Gomer Pyle's beloved Sgt. Carter, was born Oct. 23, 1923, in Clarksville. Golly!

316. There is a wild horse and burro center in Cross Plains where these creatures may be adopted. Please, don't make a mule of yourself.

TERRIFIC TENNESSEE

317. Millington was the nation's largest inland naval base during World War II.

318. Humboldt has its own Strawberry Festival Museum, while Dayton lays claim to having made the world's longest strawberry shortcake. Both towns, along with Portland, host strawberry festivals.

319. Tennessee Meiji Gakuia, which opened in Sweetwater in 1989, is the first high school in the U.S. run by the Japanese Ministry of Education.

320. Parsons hosts "the World's Biggest Coon Hunt" each April. The raccoons are treed but not shot.

321. The biggest private or corporate real estate transaction in American history occurred at Sycamore Shoals on March 17, 1775, when the Transylvania Company paid the Cherokees silver and goods worth 10,000 pounds sterling for more than 20 million acres.

TERRIFIC TENNESSEE

322. The Ford Motor Company Glass Plant in Nashville is clearly the world's largest automobile glass plant.

323. The Erwin National Fish Hatchery hatches 15 to 25 million rainbow trout annually. That's a lot of little pots of gold for happy anglers.

324. Tennessee's first driver's license was issued to Gov. Gordon Browning in 1938. Today it is parked in the Gordon Browning Museum in McKenzie.

325. John Pope's cotton from Shelby County was proclaimed the best in the world by judges at the 1851 London Crystal Palace Exhibition.

326. Millersville is home of the Museum of Beverage Containers and Advertising, where more than 30,000 different beer and soda cans lie in state. I'll drink to that.

327. Hartsville boasts the world's largest sundial.

TERRIFIC TENNESSEE

328. Sharon Stone and Rob Morrow spent part of 1995 in Nashville making the Bruce Beresford-directed film *The Last Dance*. Some scenes were filmed in the old Tennessee state pen.

329. Pulaski is home to the Giles County Dinner Theater, the only dinner theater in the world in a bank, the First National Bank.

330. The Memphis Police Museum on Beale Street is the only museum in the country that houses a working police precinct. Quite an arresting site.

331. They're not kidding around in Millington. Each September the town is home to the Goat Days International Family Festival, where, among other things, they select a Miss Nanny.

332. Morristown is the only city in the country with elevated second-floor sidewalks in its downtown business district.

TERRIFIC TENNESSEE

333. There is a Bird Dog Museum in Grand Junction, Tennessee, which highlights the talents of 36 distinct breeds of bird dogs and houses the Field Trial Hall of Fame. The National Field Trials are held in Grand Junction at Ames Plantation, beginning the second Monday of February each year.

334. Horse race history was made at the North Memphis Driving Park in 1903 when the sensational Dan Patch was clocked at 1:55 in the mile. He was ridden by Ed "Pop" Geers, a native of Wilson County, who died while horse racing at age 73.

335. Born May 18, 1909, in Cocke County, Homer Harris was a seven-foot cowboy of radio, film and television. His horse Stardust could pick Harris's Martin guitar with its nose. That's no horse tale.

336. Tennessee soil was the fighting grounds for more Civil War battles than any other state except Virginia.

TERRIFIC TENNESSEE

337. The Abraham Lincoln Museum on the campus of Harrogate's Lincoln Memorial University has the third largest collection of Lincoln and Civil War memorabilia in the world. One of the items on display is the ebony cane Lincoln took with him to Ford's Theater the night he was shot.

338. The nation's largest community of independent artists and craftsmen is the Great Smoky Arts and Crafts Community near Gatlinburg.

339. Tennessee borders eight other states, a record tied with Missouri. From atop Lookout Mountain at Chattanooga it is possible to spy seven states: Tennessee, Georgia, Alabama, North Carolina, South Carolina, Kentucky and Virginia.

340. Nationally syndicated columnist Carl T. Rowan was born Aug. 11, 1925, in Ravenscroft and grew up in McMinnville.

TERRIFIC TENNESSEE

341. John Chisum, the largest cattle baron in the U.S. in the 1870s and the subject of the John Wayne film *Chisum*, was born in 1824 in Hardeman County. He had a lot of long little dogies.

342. Hundred Oaks Castle near Winchester once maintained a library that was an exact replica of the library in Sir Walter Scott's castle in Scotland.

343. Elizabethton native Samuel Carter is the only man in American history to reach the ranks of major general (1865) and rear admiral (before retirement in 1882).

344. The first two Tennesseans to make a record were Charley Oaks and George Reneau, two blind Knoxville street singers who played guitar and harmonica. They recorded in New York for Vocalion in 1924.

345. Cedars of Lebanon State Park features the largest red cedar forest in the U.S.

346. Tusculum College, founded in Greeneville in 1794, is the oldest college in the state.

347. Born in Chattanooga on April 5, 1908, plump character comedian Grady Sutton starred in *The Boy Friends*, a series of comedy shorts directed by George Stevens in the 1930s. He made many flicks including *You Can't Cheat an Honest Man, The Bank Dick, My Man Godfrey, White Christmas, Jumbo* and *My Fair Lady*.

348. Howdee! The Grand Ole Opry's grand ole comedienne Minnie Pearl was born Sarah Ophelia Colley in Centerville on Oct. 25, 1912. The price tag on her hat read $1.98, but Cousin Minnie was priceless.

349. In 1918 Margaret Winston Caldwell, well known as a suffragist, prohibitionist and Democrat, became the first woman in the nation to own an automobile dealership with the Nashville Buick Company. She had a lot of drive.

TERRIFIC TENNESSEE

350. Since 1953, the University of Tennessee football team has had a live blue tick coon hound as its mascot. The present mascot, Smokey VII, like his predecessors, is famous for leading the Big Orange out of the giant "T" before each home game. However, the players must watch where they step.

351. The National Knife Museum in Chattanooga contains thousands of knives, swords and razors. It is also the sharpest place in the state and beloved by machairologists.

352. Moon Pies were first made in Chattanooga in 1917. How many Moon Pies would it take to reach the moon? 2,946,240,000. The Chattanooga Bakery Company now bakes about 300,000 Moon Pies per day.

353. The state tree is the tulip poplar, which makes the poplar popular.

TERRIFIC TENNESSEE

354. Cybill Shepherd has moonlighted back and forth as a TV and film star. Born in Memphis on Feb. 18, 1949, her film credits include *The Last Picture Show, The Heartbreak Kid, Taxi Driver* and *Texasville*, while her TV series include *Moonlighting, The Yellow Rose* and *Cybill*. She owns a house overlooking the Mississippi.

355. The Odd Fellows' Lodge No. 72, I.O.O.F. of Gap Creek used to meet in Hyder's Cave near Milligan in Carter County. Definitely odd fellows.

356. *Roots* author Alex Haley, who spent his youth in Henning, won a Pulitzer Prize for his novel in 1976. He also penned *The Autobiography of Malcolm X*. His boyhood home in Henning is the first state-owned historic site devoted to an African American in Tennessee. Haley's ancestor Chicken George is buried in the Bethlehem Cemetery nearby.

357. The state folk dance is the square dance.

TERRIFIC TENNESSEE

358. Roan Mountain is famous for its bald peak, a treeless summit at the 6,285-foot elevation.

359. The host of the popular early 1950s TV show *Your Hit Parade*, Snooky Lanson, was born March 27, 1914, in Memphis.

360. Charlton Heston has twice portrayed Andrew Jackson onscreen, in *The Buccaneer* and *The President's Lady*. The latter film had its world premiere in Nashville in 1953 with Heston as guest of honor.

361. William Walker, who was born in Nashville May 8, 1824, was known as "the Gray-eyed Man of Destiny" and became the president of Nicaragua in 1856.

362. Female pro baseball pitcher Jackie Mitchell struck out Babe Ruth and Lou Gehrig during an exhibition game in Chattanooga in the 1930s.

TERRIFIC TENNESSEE

363. Tennesseans became the first governors of Arkansas (John Sevier Conway), Texas (Sam Houston) and California (Peter Hardeman Burnett).

364. Knoxville, Kingston, Murfreesboro and Nashville have all served as state capitals.

365. Tom Mix spent his boyhood years in South Pittsburg before he became one of the silent screen's most famous cowboy heroes.

366. The headquarters of Cracker Barrel Country Restaurants is Lebanon, where the first Cracker Barrel opened in the Leeville community in 1969. Today there are more than 250 Cracker Barrels serving pinto beans and cornbread as good as Grandma's.

367. Memphis's Elmwood Cemetery is the final resting place of 18 Confederate generals and Kit Dalton of the Dalton brothers and James and Younger gangs.

TERRIFIC TENNESSEE

368. In 1872 Nashville barber Sampson W. Keeble became the first African American elected to the Tennessee General Assembly.

369. The Stokely brothers formed a canning company in 1898 near Newport and began selling their surplus veggies by canning 4,000 cases of tomatoes, shipping them to Knoxville and Chattanooga on the French Broad River.

370. Chattanooga is home to Dragon Dreams, a museum which boasts over 2,000 dragons on display in eight rooms. No smoking dragons allowed.

371. Actress Polly Bergen was born July 14, 1930, in Knoxville and won an Emmy in 1957 for *The Helen Morgan Story*. Polly want an Emmy.

372. Yorkville hosts an international washer pitchin' contest in August, which is far more fun than a pitcher washin' contest.

373. Wynnewood in Castalian Springs, which is two stories tall and 142 feet long, is probably the largest pioneer log structure in the state.

374. A beech tree that once stood near Reedy Creek six miles north of Johnson City bore the knife-carved inscription: "D.Boon cilled a Bar on Tree in the yEAR 1760."

375. The first rock 'n' roll record was cut at Sam Phillips's Sun Studios in Memphis in 1952. A ton of blues legends began their careers at Sun, like B.B. King, Muddy Waters and Howlin' Wolf, while some cool cats named Presley, Lewis, Cash and Perkins also had their day in the Sun.

376. The fastest mile ever recorded by a four-man team while walking on hands took place March 15, 1987, in Knoxville when David Lutterman, Danny Scannell, Philip Savage and Brendan Price covered the distance in 24 minutes, 48 seconds. They're winners, hands down.

377. Sondra Locke, who was born May 28, 1947, in Shelbyville, was nominated for an Oscar for her work in her first film, *The Heart Is a Lonely Hunter*. She later worked in many Clint Eastwood films, such as *The Gauntlet, Every Which Way but Loose, Sudden Impact* and *Bronco Billy*.

378. The world's oldest nuclear reactor, the graphite reactor built during the Manhattan Project, is a national historic landmark in Oak Ridge.

379. Bradley County is known as "the Range Capital of the World" because of its three stove manufacturers: Magic Chef, Hardwick Stove and Brown Stove Works. More ranges are produced in Cleveland than in any other city in the world. They're definitely home on the range.

380. Shelbyville has more horse sense than any other town in the state. It is home to the Tennessee Walking Horse National Celebration, which draws more than 250,000 spectators the 10 days before Labor Day.

381. University of Tennessee alumnus (class of 1910) Clarence Brown directed seven Greta Garbo films. Among his other credits are *The Yearling, Intruder in the Dust, The Human Comedy, National Velvet* and *It's a Big Country.*

382. The first railroad bridge to cross the Mississippi from Memphis, the Frisco Bridge, was opened May 12, 1892. In 1909 the Harahan Bridge was Memphis's first bridge built across the river for motor vehicles.

383. Tennessee was the last Confederate state to secede from the Union and the first to re-enter.

384. John Clemens arrived in Jamestown with his family in 1827 and served as Fentress County's first circuit court clerk and also as attorney general. Although one of his sons who became famous was born in Missouri, it is fitting that Jamestown is the site of Mark Twain Springs Park.

TERRIFIC TENNESSEE

385. Hugh Beaumont, who portrayed Ward Cleaver, the TV father of Beaver and Wally Cleaver, was a graduate of the University of Chattanooga.

386. Mary Harry Treadwell and Georgia Harry of Memphis were the first women in the U.S. to start their own insurance company.

387. Phil Harris, an alumnus of Nashville's Hume-Fogg High School, was famous as a singer, bandleader and comic. He once said, "Nashville is the best hometown in the world."

388. Gatlinburg has been called "the Honeymoon Capital of the South." In 1995 more than 10,000 couples were married there. Thus it is also "the Knot-tying Capital of the South."

389. Tom Cruise and Gene Hackman cruised Memphis in 1992 when they filmed *The Firm* there.

TERRIFIC TENNESSEE

390. The Dumas Walker (King of Marbles) Rolley Hole World championship is held every summer in Celina. The late Walker was made famous in a song by the Kentucky HeadHunters. The world's first marble festival, the International Marble Festival, was held Sept. 13-14, 1996, at Standing Stone State Park near Livingston.

391. Al Geiberger became the first PGA golfer to break 60 in a tournament when he shot a 59 at the Danny Thomas Classic on Memphis's Colonial Golf Club course June 10, 1977.

392. Three northeastern Tennessee counties formed the independent State of Franklin from 1784 to 1788, with John Sevier as governor. North Carolina regained control of the area in 1788, and it has since been known as "the Lost State of Franklin."

393. Austin Peay was the only Tennessee governor to die in office.

TERRIFIC TENNESSEE

394. Memphis was home to the American Snuff plant, which in the 1930s was the largest strong snuff factory in America. Snuff said.

395. The first black church in the state was Nashville's First Baptist Church Colored, established in 1848.

396. The Opryland Hotel Convention Center is the largest hotel east of the Mississippi River.

397. George Hamilton filled the shoes of Hank Williams Sr. in the 1964 flick *Your Cheatin' Heart*, which was shot in Nashville. Years later, Richard Thomas came to Music City to play Hank Williams Jr. in the TV movie *Living Proof*.

398. Headquarters of the Southern Baptist Association, Nashville has more than 700 churches of all denominations.

TERRIFIC TENNESSEE

399. Gibson County has the oldest continuously held fair in the South. They've been going to the fair there since October 1856. That's a lot of cotton candy down the hatch.

400. Loretta Lynn's Ranch in Hurricane Mills draws more than 400,000 dudes annually.

401. Goodness gracious! Country music wild man Jerry Lee Lewis saw his life story come to the silver screen in *Great Balls of Fire*, which was filmed in Memphis in 1988.

402. Two of TV's four *Designing Women* are Tennessee natives. Dixie Carter was born May 25, 1939, in McLemoresville, while Annie Potts was born Oct. 28, 1952, in Nashville.

403. The longest neon sign in the world is the letter M on the Mississippi River Bridge in Memphis. The M is 1,800 feet long.

404. John Sevier, known as Nolichucky Jack, was governor of the "lost" state of Franklin, governor of the state of Tennessee for six terms and elected U.S. Congressman from Tennessee four times.

405. The Little Debbie Snack Cakes, the top snack cake brand in the country, first came out of the oven in 1960. Made by McKee Foods in Collegedale, Little Debbies were named after a granddaughter of the founder, O.D. McKee.

406. The newly freed slaves of Baltimore gave a special Bible to President Lincoln on July 4, 1864, at the White House in appreciation of his part in their emancipation. One of the most famous artifacts in African-American history, it was given to Fisk University in 1916 by Lincoln's son, Robert Todd Lincoln.

407. The Sam Houston Schoolhouse near Maryville, built in 1794, is the oldest school building in Tennessee.

TERRIFIC TENNESSEE

408. McMinnville native Dottie West became the first country music singer to record a national jingle when she sang about country sunshine for Coca-Cola. Dottie was the real thing.

409. When Tennessee seceded from the Union, Scott County voted against separation, passed a resolution seceding from the state and formed the Free and Independent State of Scott. Great Scott!

410. In 1935 the Long Island of the Holston was one of the first places in America to be designated a national historic landmark. It was on this "island of peace" in 1776 that Dr. Patrick Vance discovered a method of treating victims of scalpings.

411. Michael Jeter, who was born Aug. 26, 1951, in Lawrenceburg, won a Tony Award in 1992 for *Grand Hotel* and an Emmy Award in 1991 for his role of Herman Stiles on *Evening Shade*.

TERRIFIC TENNESSEE

412. The world record for sweating off excess pounds in 24 hours was set in Nashville in August 1984 when Ron Allen perspired off 21.5 pounds. Move over Weight Watchers.

413. Every summer around the first week of June, over 24,000 country music fanatics crowd into Nashville for Fan Fair, where they meet and greet their favorite singers and have the opportunity to snap photographs and get their autographs.

414. The Tennessee State Museum in Nashville features such items as Davy Crockett's rifle, Andrew Jackson's top hat, Daniel Boone's musket, Andrew Johnson's piano, James K. Polk's walking cane, Sam Davis's boot and Sam Houston's guitar. You see 'em in the museum.

415. Knoxville native Adolph S. Ochs bought the *New York Times* in 1896 and invented the slogan "All the news that's fit to print."

416. Sissy Spacek has made three feature films in the state: she portrayed Loretta Lynn and sang just like her in *Coal Miner's Daughter* (1980); she starred opposite Mel Gibson in *The River* (1983), which was filmed in and around Kingsport, Rogersville and Bristol; and she played real-life whistleblower Marie Ragghianti in *Marie* (1984).

417. The world's first antique mall was opened in Lebanon in the mid-1960s by Rusty Price.

418. Twice a year Diana's all-night gospel singings near Pulaski in Giles County draw as many as two to three thousand acapella singers from more than 20 states. Begun in 1969, the hymn fest is held the second weekend of June and September.

419. The first novel printed in the state was *Woodville* (1832, in Knoxville), which was penned by the state's first novelist, Charles Todd.

TERRIFIC TENNESSEE

420. Born in Montgomery County in 1861, Elizabeth (Meriwether) Gilmer, who used the pen name Dorothy Dix, was one of America's first advice columnists. She also wrote the book *How To Win and Hold a Husband*.

421. Because of its many nurseries and orchards, Warren County has been called "the Nursery Capital of the South."

422. The Ocoee Flume, a five-mile-long wooden flume, is the largest structure of its type in the U.S. When the 1996 Olympics canoeing and kayaking events were held on the Ocoee River, it was the first time a natural river was used for those events.

423. One of the largest stalagmites in the world can be seen in Cudjo's Cave at the Cumberland Gap National Park. At 35 feet in circumference and 65 feet high, the formation is estimated to be 85 million years old, give or take a few years.

TERRIFIC TENNESSEE

424. John Lee "Sonny Boy" Williamson, famous for his blues harmonica and especially the tune *Good Morning Little Schoolgirl*, was born March 30, 1914, in Jackson.

425. Nashville's Hadley Park (1912) is believed to be the nation's first public park established for African-American citizens.

426. Among other interesting items, the Lenoir Museum features a collection of mousetraps. Say cheese!

427. Bluegrass music legend Lester Flatt, half of Flatt & Scruggs, was born in Overton County on June 28, 1914, and lived most of his life in Sparta. Flatt was pretty sharp.

428. During the Civil War, the Hunt-Phelan Home in Memphis was the headquarters of Gen. U.S. Grant, as was Magnolia Manor in Bolivar and Cherry Mansion in Savannah.

429. Dixie Gun Works in Union City is the world's largest supplier of antique guns and parts.

TERRIFIC TENNESSEE

430. In 1794 the first map of Tennessee was made by Gen. Daniel Smith, for whom Smith County was named. Smith, who built Rock Castle in Hendersonville, is credited with giving the state its name.

431. *Wild River*, starring Montgomery Clift, Lee Remick and Jo Van Fleet, was filmed in and around Charleston, Cleveland and Calhoun in 1959.

432. In 1966 Waylon Jennings starred in *Nashville Rebel* and performed that tune along with *Nashville Bum*. Others in the flick included Tex Ritter, singing *Hillbilly Heaven*, comic Henny Youngman and Loretta Lynn.

433. The record attendance for a women's college basketball game is 24,563, which was set Dec. 9, 1987, when the University of Tennessec took on the University of Texas in Knoxville.

434. The state butterfly is the zebra swallowtail.

TERRIFIC TENNESSEE

435. Sneedville's Old Jail is being remodeled to become the first Melungeon Museum of History and Culture. The Melungeons, unique to Hancock County, are believed to be of Mediterranean stock with Arabic, Berber, Portuguese and Spanish heritage.

436. Nashville's Ryman Auditorium, "the Mother Church of Country Music," was opened in 1892 by riverboat captain Thomas Ryman as a religious tabernacle and was home of the Grand Ole Opry from 1943 to 1974.

437. Both Polk County and Cosby host Ramp Festivals in the spring. The wild, onion-like plant has been called "the sweetest-tasting, vilest-smelling plant" that grows. Don't forget the Certs.

438. The youngest man to serve in the House of Representatives was Jeffersonian Democrat William Charles Cole Claiborne, who was elected to his seat in August 1797 at the age of 22.

TERRIFIC TENNESSEE

439. Shannon Doherty of *Beverly Hills, 90210* fame was born April 12, 1971, in Memphis.

440. Eastman Chemical, formerly part of Eastman Kodak, is the largest industrial employer in the state with 13,000 employees in Kingsport. Quite a development.

441. Tennessee is the only Southern state that mines copper, all of which comes from Polk County.

442. Carbo's Smoky Mountain Police Museum in Pigeon Forge has on display the 1974 Corvette in which Buford Pusser died, along with the actual "Big Stick" and all the badges used in the *Walking Tall* films.

443. *A Walk in the Spring Rain*, starring Ingrid Bergman and Anthony Quinn, was filmed in Gatlinburg, Cades Cove and on the campus of the University of Tennessee at Knoxville in 1970. It was based on the novel by Tennessee author Rachel Maddux.

444. Tom Jager became the fastest swimmer in history when he hit an average of 5.37 miles per hour over a distance of 50 yards in a 25-yard pool in Nashville on March 23, 1990.

445. Essyngton in Robertson County is the oldest and largest farm in the nation to be continuously owned and operated by one family (1819).

446. Nashville's Jordanaires have performed on more No. 1 hits than any other vocal group in the world.

447. The Ku Klux Klan was started on Christmas Eve 1865 in Pulaski by Judge T.M. Jones and his son Calvin. It began as a social club. The Grand Cyclops, Gen. Nathan Bedford Forrest, disbanded the group in March 1869.

448. RCA's Studio B is the only remaining original Music Row studio in Nashville. Among the many greats who recorded there have been Elvis Presley and Dolly Parton.

TERRIFIC TENNESSEE

449. The National Catfish Derby is held every summer in Savannah below Pickwick Dam on the Tennessee River.

450. American playwright Thomas Lanier Williams chose his pen name of Tennessee Williams because of fond memories of his early childhood in Nashville.

451. Double Cola was invented in Chattanooga in 1927 by Charles Little, and in 1934 he produced the first soft drink bottle with a painted label. Today Double Cola is also bottled in Moscow, Russia.

452. The Overmountain Men of the Watauga and Nolichucky Valleys set up the first free and independent government in America when they met in the Watauga Assembly in May 1772.

453. The University of Tennessee was established in 1794 and underwent three name changes (from Blount College to East Tennessee College to East Tennessee University) before it became UT in 1879.

TERRIFIC TENNESSEE

454. Filmed in Townsend, the TV series *Christy* was based on the novel by Catherine Marshall which tells of her mother, Leonora Wood, an Appalachian schoolteacher.

455. Super UT football fan and actor David Keith was born in Knoxville on May 8, 1954. His film credits include *The Great Santini, An Officer and a Gentleman, The Lords of Discipline*, and *The Two Jakes*. He played Elvis in *Heartbreak Hotel* in 1989.

456. One of Hollywood's all-time great choreographers, Hermes Pan was born in Memphis. Because of his physical resemblance to Fred Astaire, he often doubled for the star in film and he worked on 17 films with Astaire. Pan won an Oscar in 1937 for *A Damsel in Distress* and an Emmy in 1959 for *An Evening With Fred Astaire*. Among his many film credits are *The Gay Divorcee, Porgy and Bess, Can-Can, Flower Drum Song, The Pink Panther, Cleopatra* and *My Fair Lady*.

TERRIFIC TENNESSEE

457. A crater near Well's Creek in Stewart County is nine miles in diameter, making it the third largest in the U.S.

458. Discovered beneath the Jacob Burkle Estate in Memphis is a series of tunnels with the only known remaining tracks from the Underground Railway.

459. The first monument in memory of an unknown soldier of the Confederacy was erected in Union City in 1869.

460. University of Tennessee coach Pat Summitt has won four NCAA women's basketball titles and an Olympic gold medal (1984) during her career. She also won an Olympic silver medal as a player in 1976.

461. Gatlinburg's Christus Gardens, claiming to be America's No. 1 religious attraction, is the site of the famed Marble Face of Christ, the most photographed single object in Gatlinburg. No matter where you stand, the eyes of Jesus follow you.

TERRIFIC TENNESSEE

462. Nissan pickup trucks are manufactured only in Smyrna. Its Nissan plant is the largest automobile factory in the U.S. with a building that covers 5.1 million square feet.

463. Two 60-foot-tall King Kongs took over Pigeon Forge in 1986 for the filming of *King Kong Lives*. The place went ape.

464. The Tennessee River is 652 miles long, while the Cumberland River rolls along for 687 miles.

465. Crockett County, named after David, changed the name of its county seat from Cageville to Alamo after the famous fight in Texas. Remember?

466. Among the most popular songs with a Tennessee connection in the title are *Tennessee River* by Alabama, *Tennessee Stud* by Eddy Arnold, *Tennessee Waltz* by Patti Page and *Chattanooga Choo-Choo* by Glenn Miller, which was the first "gold record."

TERRIFIC TENNESSEE

467. Piggly Wiggly commenced in Memphis in 1916 when Clarence Saunders conceived of a self-service grocery market. A replica of that first store may be seen at the Memphis Pink Palace Museum.

468. Folks at Smithville gets to fiddlin' around every year near the Fourth of July 'cause that's when they host their famous Fiddlers' Jamboree.

469. Olan Mills, founded in 1932, has had its headquarters in Chattanooga since 1942. The nation's family portrait giant shoots over 10 million smiles a year.

470. Astronomer Edward E. Barnard, a Nashville native and Vanderbilt grad, discovered Jupiter's fifth moon in 1892 and found 16 comets. He was a pioneer of celestial photography, which means he really shot the moon.

471. The nation's first officially recorded butterfat test was conducted in 1889 by Columbia's Major W.J. Webster.

TERRIFIC TENNESSEE

472. Franklin driver Darrell Waltrip was the Winston Cup trophy winner in 1981, 1982 and 1985. The racecar driver owns a Honda dealership in Franklin.

473. Six Confederate generals were killed in one day during the battle of Franklin. Four of the bodies were brought to Carnton, a mansion named by the builder for his father's hometown of Cairntown, Ireland. The name means "where the warriors are buried," which proved prophetic since it was constructed 35 years before the Civil War.

474. The Parthenon in Nashville's Centennial Park is the only replica of the original in Athens, Greece, and houses Athena, the tallest indoor sculpture in the Western world. Memphis has the third largest pyramid in the world, which is built of glass and steel.

475. Singer-songwriter Dave Loggins of *Please Come to Boston* fame was born Nov. 10, 1947, in Mountain City. Who's the No. 1 fan of the man from Tennessee?

TERRIFIC TENNESSEE

476. Greeneville tailor Andrew Johnson held elective office at the local, state and federal level that included alderman, mayor, state representative, state senator, governor, U.S. congressman, senator, vice president and president. Johnson never went to school. One of the last official acts of the seventeenth president was to pardon all Southerners who had fought in the Civil War.

477. With five acres of slippery, Ober Gatlinburg's ski resort has the world's largest artificial skiing surface. That's some snow job.

478. Lauderdale County, known as "the Tomato Capital of the South," hosts a tomato festival each July in Ripley, believe it or not.

479. Skullbone in Gibson County, also billed as "the Kingdom of Skullbonia," was named after skullbone boxing, where men would swap punches to the head until only one remained standing.

TERRIFIC TENNESSEE

480. The Great Smoky Mountains National Park is the most visited of all the national parks. They're really smokin'.

481. The Parthenon features the largest bronze doors in the world. Don't knock it.

482. The first white men to cross into Tennessee over the Appalachian Mountains were James Needham and Gabriel Arthur in 1673.

483. Nashvillian Hugh Mott was a second lieutenant in March 1945 when he led his platoon from the village of Remagen across the Ledendorf bridge under heavy fire to save it for the advancing Allied forces. This turning point in WWII was chronicled by Hollywood in the film *The Bridge at Remagen*.

484. Nashville pro golfer Lou Graham made more than a million dollars from the PGA Tour and won the U.S. Open in 1975.

TERRIFIC TENNESSEE

485. Chattanooga means "rock coming to a point" and refers to Lookout Mountain.

486. The state rock is limestone, while the state stone is agate.

487. Tennessee became the 16th state in the Union on June 1, 1796.

488. Chattanooga tennis pro Roscoe Tanner was quite an ace at his sport. He was famous for his serve which whistled across the net at up to 140 miles per hour.

489. Christopher Jones, who starred in the title role of TV's *The Legend of Jesse James* in 1965, was born in Jackson Aug. 18, 1941.

490. Nashville scientist Jack DeWitt was the first man to establish radar contact with the moon.

491. Tennessee is 432 miles long and 106 miles wide.

TERRIFIC TENNESSEE

492. David Lipscomb University in Nashville has produced the two all-time leading scorers in college basketball: John Pierce (4,230 points, class of 1994) and Philip Hutcheston (4,106, class of 1990). The Bison ball team's Andy McQueen is the NAIA's all-time three-point shooter with 515 treys and Marcus Bodie is the NAIA all-time steal leader with 440 career swipes.

493. Knoxville's Patricia Neal won an Oscar for best actress in 1963 for *Hud*.

494. "What the thoroughfare of Wall Street will do to you if you don't know a stock, Columbia will do to you if you don't know a mule." Thus saith Will Rogers on the status of Columbia as "the Mule Capital of the World."

495. There are many towns named Greenville across the U.S., but only Tennessee's spells Greeneville with an "e" in the middle.

496. The largest bicycle factory in the world is in Lawrenceburg.

TERRIFIC TENNESSEE

497. For more than two years, Lady, a mongrel from Tullahoma, wrote a weekly advice column for dog owners in the *National Examiner*. She also wrote a book, *The Gospel According to Lady*, and ran for the Presidency in 1980 with the slogan "It's better for a dog to go to the White House than for the White House to go to the dogs." Lady had a human secretary in Charles Stoney Jackson.

498. Director Sam Raimi, whose other works include the films *Darkman* and *The Quick and the Dead* and the TV series *Hercules* and *American Gothic*, directed his first film in Morristown in 1979 where he also blew up a bridge. The film, *The Evil Dead*, has been called by critic Leonard Maltin "the grossest horror film ever."

499. The gunboat that fired the first shot of the Spanish-American War was the *Nashville*.

500. Grainger County boasts the oldest standing brick jail in the state. It was built in 1848.

TERRIFIC TENNESSEE

501. Stella Stevens grew up in Memphis and starred in *The Nutty Professor, The Silencers, The Poseidon Adventure* and *The Ballad of Cable Hogue.* Her son, actor Andrew Stevens, was born in Memphis on June 10, 1955.

502. The world's first lunch box collectors' convention, the Box-A-Rama, was held in Oak Ridge in 1990.

503. Of the 180 men who died at the Alamo, 33 of them were Tennessee volunteers, including David Crockett and James Bowie.

504. Complete circular rainbows have been seen atop Roan Mountain. No pot of gold there.

505. Born in Roane County in 1882, Sam Rayburn spent 17 years as Speaker of the House, the longest any man ever held the position.

TERRIFIC TENNESSEE

506. Elizabeth Patterson, born in Savannah in 1875 and buried in Savannah Cemetery, was a silent film star of the 1920s who went on to appear in the talkies *Tom Sawyer, Tobacco Road, Intruder in the Dust, Alexander the Great* and more than 90 other films. The star of Broadway plays also performed on TV as Mrs. Trumbull, the babysitter on *I Love Lucy*.

507. Ethridge is home of Granny Evett's TV Network, a 10-watt station that is one of the smallest TV stations in the country. Stop by her Lawrenceburg studio around 2 p.m. weekdays and she'll make you a star for two minutes.

508. Jonesborough, which was founded on Jan. 17, 1779, is the oldest permanent European settlement in Tennessee and has been nicknamed "the Mother of Tennessee." Trade, near Mountain City, is the state's oldest unincorporated community (1673).

509. For a Tennessee vacation guide, call 1-800-491-TENN.

Selected References

The Aviation History of Tennessee, Jim Fulbright, Tennessee Department of Transportation, Aeronautics Division, 1996

An Encyclopedia of East Tennessee, edited by Jim Stokely and Jeff D. Johnson, Children's Museum of Oak Ridge, 1981

The Encyclopedia of Tennessee, Somerset Publishers, Inc., 1993

The Film Encyclopedia, Ephraim Katz, HarperPerennial, 1994

The Guinness Book of Records, Bantam Books, 1995

Historical Reminiscences of Carter County, Tennessee, edited by Mildred Kozsuch, The Overmountain Press, 1985

History of Tennessee, Stanley J. Folmsbee, Robert E. Corlew and Enoch L. Mitchell, Lewis Historical Publishing Company, Inc. 1960

Horizons of Tennessee, David A. Bice and Jessie Shields Strickland, Walsworth Publishing Company Inc., 1989

The Lebanon Democrat, various issues

The Nashville Banner, various issues

The Overmountain Men, Pat Alderman, The Overmountain Press, 1986

Reflections and Images, Tennessee Extension Homemakers Council, 1986

Roan Mountain: A Passage of Time, Jennifer Bauer Wilson, John F. Blair Publisher, 1991

The TV Encyclopedia, David Inman, Perigee Books, 1991

The Tennessean, various issues

The Tennessee Almanac and Book of Facts, James A. Crutchfield, Rutledge Hill Press, 1986

The Tennessee Blue Book, State of Tennessee, 1995

Tennessee, A Chronology and Documentary Handbook, Robert I. Vexler, Oceana Publication Inc., 1979

Tennessee Heritage, David J. Harkness, The University of Tennessee Continuing Education Series, 1971

The Tennessee Magazine, various issues

Tennessee, Off the Beaten Path, Tim O'Brien, Globe Pequot Press, 1993

The Tennessee Sampler, Peter Jenkins and Friends, Thomas Nelson Publishers, 1985

Tennessee State Symbols, Rob Simbeck, Altheus Press, 1995

Tennessee Taproots, Sophie and Paul Crane, Earle-Shields Publishers, 1976

Tennessee and Tennesseans, Bethenia McLemore Oldham, 1903

Tennessee Then and Now, Harry M. Joiner, Southern Textbook Publisher, Inc., 1983

The Tennessee Department of Tourist Development, various publications

The Tennessee Film, Entertainment & Music Commission, various publications, 1993

Touring the East Tennessee Backroads, Carolyn Sakowski, John F. Blair Publishers, 1993

The WPA Guide to Tennessee, The University of Tennessee Press, Federal Writers' Project, State of Tennessee, 1939, 1986

The World Almanac of the U.S.A., World Almanac Book, Allan Carpenter and Carl Provorse, 1993

Your Tennessee, Jesse Burt, Steck-Vaughn Company, 1974

If your favorite gift shop or bookstore is out of
TERRIFIC TENNESSEE and you'd like to have a
couple of extra copies for the Volunteers in your life, you
can order through the mail by sending a check or money
order made payable to PREMIUM PRESS AMERICA
in the amount of $8.95 ($6.95 plus $2.00 shipping).

> **TERRIFIC TENNESSEE**
> PREMIUM PRESS AMERICA
> P.O. Box 159015
> Nashville, TN 37215
> (800) 891-7323
> (615) 256-8484

For additional copies . . .

> 2 books: $11.95 plus $2.00 shipping = $13.95
> 3 books: $15.95 plus $2.00 shipping = $17.95
> 4 books: $18.95 plus $2.00 shipping = $20.95

Allow 2 weeks for delivery.